ABANDONED
CINCINNATI

SAMUEL WRIGHT SMITH

America Through Time is an imprint of Fonthill Media LLC
www.through-time.com
office@through-time.com

Published by Arcadia Publishing by arrangement with Fonthill Media LLC
For all general information, please contact Arcadia Publishing:
Telephone: 843-853-2070
Fax: 843-853-0044
E-mail: sales@arcadiapublishing.com
For customer service and orders:
Toll-Free 1-888-313-2665

www.arcadiapublishing.com

First published 2020

Copyright © Samuel Wright Smith 2020

ISBN 978-1-63499-248-0

All rights reserved. No part of this publication may be reproduced, stored in a retrieval system or transmitted in any form or by any means, electronic, mechanical, photocopying, recording or otherwise, without prior permission in writing from Fonthill Media LLC

Typeset in Trade Gothic 10pt on 15pt
Printed and bound in England

CONTENTS

Acknowledgments   **4**

Introduction   **5**

1   The U.S. Playing Card Factory   **7**

2   Lincoln Heights Elementary School   **19**

3   Lincoln Heights YMCA   **23**

4   First German Reformed Church   **30**

5   Americana Amusement Park/LeSourdsville Lake   **41**

6   Kennedy Heights Jr. High School   **50**

7   Loveland Predestinarian Baptist Church   **61**

8   Quantum Chemicals Research Division   **66**

9   The Crosley Building   **76**

10   Peters Cartridge Factory   **84**

About the Author   **96**

ACKNOWLEDGMENTS

Thank you to everyone who helped make this book possible, through monetary support or otherwise. I'd like to extend a special thank you to Brighton Hummer, Carolan Glatstein, Claire Beseler, David Miller/*Loveland Magazine*, Dean Parker, Emily Shaver, Isabella Huelsman, James Barrett, James McLean, Jerry Jiang, Jess Griffiths, Joe Timmerman, John Lathrop, Lauren Questell, Lori Walker, Lupin Myst, Malcolm Silver-Van Meter, Melissa Chilkotowsky, Nanette Heiser, Niki Fiorenza, Radu Vasilescu, Susan and Jon Hoffheimer and Tim Purtell.

Abandoned Cincinnati was edited by Chris Smith, David Miller, Isabella Huelsman, Sam Sauer and Jon Hoffheimer.

Dedicated to my dad, who taught me to let my heart guide my adventures and explorations.

INTRODUCTION

And then it hits me: that oh-so distinct smell.

It is the smell of wet, decaying wood. Standing water on concrete foundation. Mold, spores, lichen, asbestos. The building greets me with a fetid breath.

And then: everything the smell carries with it.

Holes in the floor and peeling paint. A mummified possum and moss-covered walls stained with wet rust. The calm of a space alive after human life. A reclaimed "gone beyond-ness."

Texture on texture. Natural order forming right-angles. A structure at once dying and being reborn.

All abandoned buildings share this life out of death. Yet, each structure hides a unique atmosphere and gestates a history. These buildings hold stories of real humans. Hands once drew music out of these keyboards and pianos. Parents sat in a middle school auditorium and boots trudged industrial stairs. These factories, amusement parks and churches are time capsules containing slices of Cincinnati's past.

The photographs in this book span six years of my work, and many of the locations are dramatically different now than when I visited. Dilapidated buildings are always in flux. They are alive. These images preserve spaces in the moment in which I found them.

Some of the shots are unconventional in the world of urban exploration photography. I am partial to celluloid film for its textural, organic randomness and unpredictability. These qualities reflect decay. Through multiple-exposure layering effects, underexposing, light-leaking and unorthodox developing techniques, I hope that the addition of experimental images helps to convey the mood of these buildings as well as their past. Although I have tried, there is no way to put words to the emotion held inside long-vacant hallways and basement boiler rooms. If I am successful, the images will speak what I cannot write.

1

THE U.S. PLAYING CARD FACTORY

The 21-acre, 470,00-square foot, eleven-building Romanesque Revival U. S. Playing Card factory is characterized from the exterior by huge semi-circle windows, curved brickwork and elegant symmetry. Designed by Samuel Hannaford and Sons, a clock tower sets the Norwood building apart. Overgrown railroad tracks lead to the rear entrance where materials were loaded and unloaded for over 100 years. A smokestack casts a shadow across a mosquito-filled reservoir now echoing with frogs.

Through a door shrouded in vines and thorns, there is a 25-foot wall of steel pipes, boilers, valves, ladders and shattered windows.

Sunlight breaks through smoke in the boiler room of the U.S. Playing Card factory.

A Bailey Fluid Meter manufactured in Cleveland, Ohio. The flow rate needle found its final resting place in 2002.

Above: One of the many water-matted stacks of steam flow graphs in the boiler room.

Right: A Westinghouse brand differential relay panel with a magnet-based graphing device. The panel is three-phased, with boards for distributing electricity to different buildings.

A skywalk connects the boiler room and the main building. Long hardwood floor hallways lead to open factory rooms. Carpeted executive and art department offices are illuminated by massive windows.

Founded in 1867, the U.S. Playing Card factory produced the ubiquitous Bicycle Playing Card deck along with the Bee, Erlanger, Hoyle and Aviator decks. Additionally, the factory created casino-specialty cards and poker chips. Construction on the Norwood facility began at the end of the 1800s and continued for over 200 years. In 2009, the company moved to Erlanger, KY, and continues to be one of the largest playing card manufacturers in the world.

U.S. Playing Cards were made with 11,000-pound rolls of paper and linen sandwiched with a special-made black glue. Cards were made on poster-sized printouts and were punched at a rate of 350 cards a minute.

Opposite above: A barrel of Nicoat, a printing and packaging coating manufactured by ICP Industrial. This was used as a varnish for the playing cards and helped make them more durable.

Opposite below: One of the many piles of punched card sheets found around the U.S. Playing Card factory.

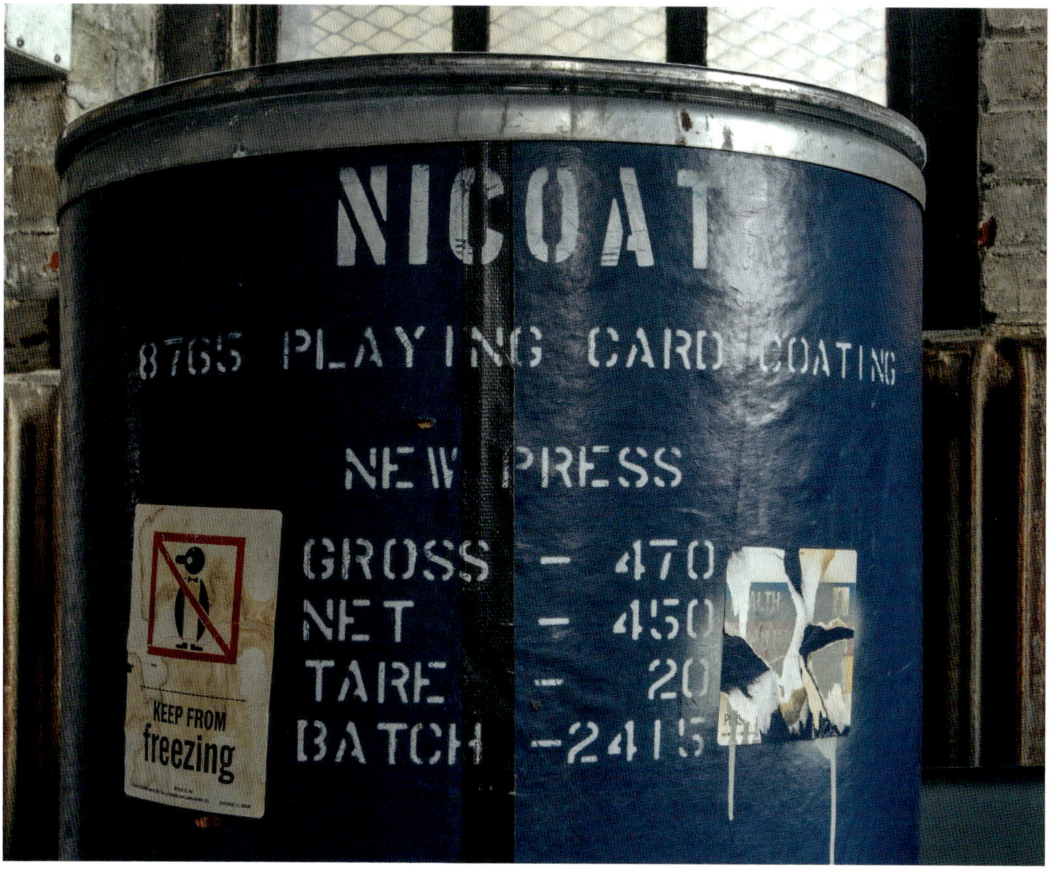
NICOAT
8765 PLAYING CARD COATING
NEW PRESS
GROSS - 470
NET - 450
TARE - 20
BATCH -2415
KEEP FROM
freezing

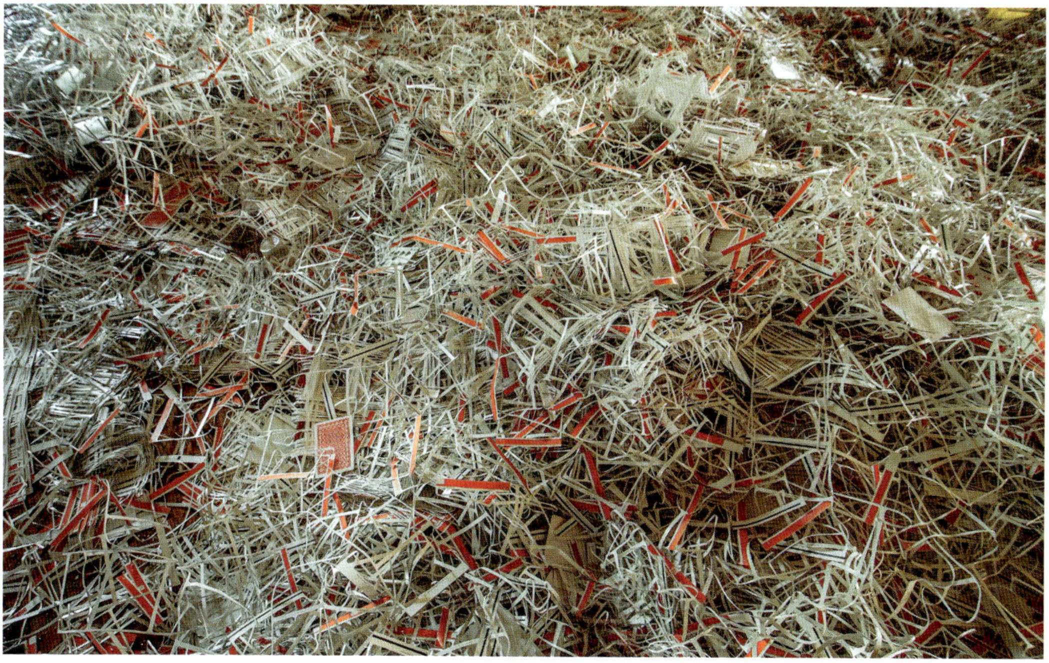

Cards that never made it to the punching machine rest on a conveyor belt.

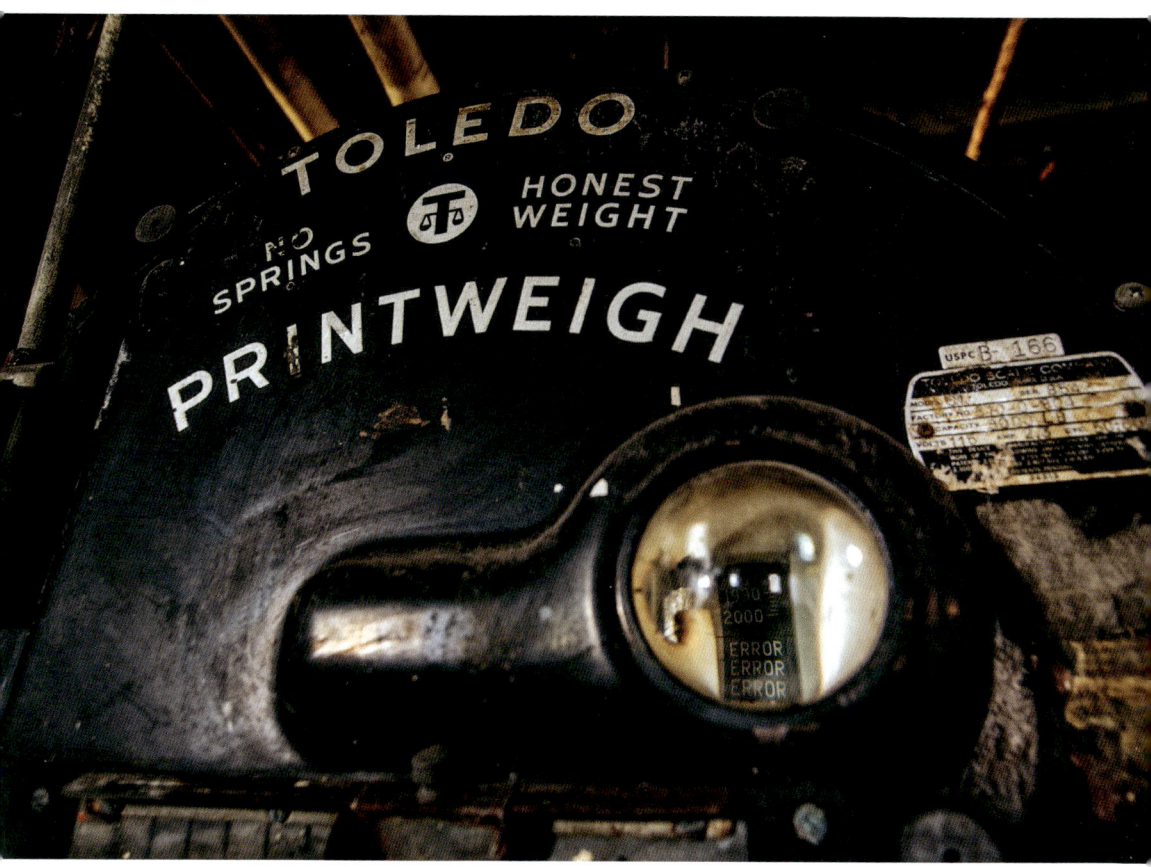

A Toledo Scale used to weigh the massive rolls of paper and other materials. Raw supplies were received by train and truck and moved here by a pulley system outside the bottom floor entrance.

    In World War II, The Red Cross delivered U.S. Playing Cards to Allied prisoners of war in Germany. When wet, the cards would peel in two and reveal a secret. Inside the cards puzzle pieces of a map revealed possible escape routes.

    Similarly, the company's cards were utilized as a tool for psychological warfare in the Vietnam War. As a result of French occupation, the Vietnamese acquired a belief of card-based fortune telling. In the tradition of card reading, an ace of spades is known as "the death card". The U.S. Playing Card Company supplied specially-made ace of spade decks bearing Lady Liberty or a skull and crossbones to soldiers. American troops scattered cards on forest floors and placed them in the mouths of dead Viet Cong soldiers.

Left: A barn swallow circles the iconic clock tower at sunset.

Below: Playing cards sit on a dusty wiring diagram in the clock tower.

The clock tower is the heart of the U.S. Playing Card factory. When fully wound, the 7-foot mechanism would run for days at a time without maintenance. A crank system moved a hanging weight that provided force to turn the clock hands. Varying sized gears allowed for a minute, second and hour hand. Subtle changes of size in the pendulum (located inside a hole in the floor) due to temperature changes would have caused a gain of time in winter and loss of time in summer.

A few years after construction, the bells were replaced by a speaker playing WSAI, an AM radio station operated out of and owned by the card factory. WSAI broadcasted bridge lessons, playing card advertisements and music. The station was eventually sold to Crosley Radio Company.

I made my way to the clock tower by a series of rusted staircases and ladders. Enclosed in the frosted-glass evening light, I found myself suspended in a strange calm. Time had stopped. The collective lifetimes that were given to keep the factory operating are hardly imaginable. Now, pulleys and gears and pendulums are embalmed in their moment of departure.

The clock heart.

Left: Mechanisms eclipse the east clock face at sunset.

Below: Gears, levers, pulleys, cranks and weights kept the entirely mechanical clock ticking over Norwood until the 2000s.

Twilight bathes warehouses and pylons.

A 35mm triple exposure of a suspended moment.

On top of the tower, curved concrete and ornate metalwork provides a sense of grandeur.

2

LINCOLN HEIGHTS ELEMENTARY SCHOOL

I stepped into a cinder block hallway painted with sunlight and found myself in someone's hazy memory. On the wall to my left, a poem about a giraffe and an art teacher's charmingly crude rendering of a kangaroo. Down the hall, low-railed stairways and informational posters.

In this new memory, the carpet has been replaced by a floor of moss. Murals peel and weeds grow from cracks where a playground once stood.

A concrete sign above the front entrance. Stylized Art-Deco font face reads 1936, the date of completion.

A wall clock that stopped at 7:46 hangs over animal paintings. Water damage has carved a river through the ceiling paint.

The village of Lincoln Heights was initially built by developers to be an unincorporated, segregated suburb lacking firefighters, police and in some areas, electricity. The originally black-only Lincoln Heights Elementary School was constructed as a part of the Woodlawn School District in 1936. The school was abandoned in 2006 upon completion of a replacement constructed due to high violence rates in the area. In 2015, the school unsuccessfully attempted to auction the building. The following year, Lincoln Heights Elementary suffered minor damage as the result of arson.

Above: A handful of teal lockers provide a looking glass to the first day of summer in 2006.

Right: Sunlight spills down rusted rails and peeling stairs.

Risers are lit by broken windows and scattered with material deemed useless by metal scrappers.

A stage bearing the motto "Tiger Pride."

3

LINCOLN HEIGHTS YMCA

Next door to Lincoln Heights Elementary, a newer, one-story building rests in a similar state of dilapidation. Opening steel double-doors: mold, sunlight, rows of lockers and fallen ceiling panels. Unbreathable, rancid, thick air. The Lincoln Heights YMCA was toxic. I would not have entered without a respirator.

Built in 1958, this building was originally the Lincoln Heights High School (LHHS) and was intended to desegregate the community. In the 2000s, Princeton, a neighboring school system, began to absorb students from LHHS. The school was eventually converted into a YMCA. An in-ground pool stood behind the YMCA but eventually developed a crack. In 2004, the pool was buried rather than repaired due to insufficient funds.

One of the most surprising discoveries in the YMCA were clothes. Shirts, pants, socks. Piles of damp garments among empty cigarette cartons. Pillows laid out as makeshift mattresses. Stuffed animals. A hallway of damp, moldy rooms like this. Not so long ago, people had lived here.

The entrance to the Lincoln Heights YMCA. The lockers are evidence of previous use as a high school.

Light falls through a hole in the ceiling on stage curtains and a basketball hoop. Water and fire damage have caused the gymnasium floor to billow and bend.

Above: A hole in the ceiling weathers a strip of stage lights.

Right: A scoreboard hangs on a mold-coated cinderblock gym wall.

A softly illuminated locker room.

A bookcase decays in front of a chalkboard.

A row of lockers lined with hand-painted depictions of Mickey Mouse.

Left: A foosball table in a recreation room.

Below: Trophies line a boarded window.

Above: The yellow-stained keys of a Wurlitzer organ. The room also contained large speakers and several bales of hay.

Right: A possum decays on a moldy carpet. Animals often find their way into abandoned buildings and become trapped.

4

FIRST GERMAN REFORMED CHURCH

Every abandoned building has a hard-to-describe yet easy-to-experience mood. In part, the soul of a building comes from its history, the objects inside and the architecture. But there is a difficult-to-define "something else."

In the grasp of overgrowth and decay, decrepit buildings do not die. Instead, they find new life. It may be the trees and moss and termites returning to their rightful places that breathes spirit into the buildings. Abandoned. But they are not vacant.

The First German Reformed Church has stood in Clifton for 150 years and for 50 it has stood vacant. The cathedral was built to provide a space of worship for the large German Cincinnati populace. In 1918, due to rising anti-German sentiments during the first World War, the church changed its name to the Freeman Avenue United Church of Christ. As the Clifton Heights population shifted culturally and economically, the church saw attendance decline. In 1970, the congregation relocated. Robes, books, cans of applesauce, flags, and pianos were left behind.

The ornate windows and shutters on the steeple of the First German Reformed Church.

The front entrance of the First German Reformed Church. The Gothic Revival style stonework and arches help to create a stunning piece of architecture.

Dusty religious books spill off broken shelves.

Religious books rest on tile. *People Who Knew God* was written by Gertrude Priester in 1964. Hundreds of books were scattered throughout the bottom floor of the church.

Piano keys ease into dust. The Ebersole Piano company was dissolved in 1909, making this piano over 100 years old.

A priest's red robe hangs on the bottom floor of the First German Reformed Church. Red robes represent the blood of martyrs and are used on Maundy Thursday and Palm Sunday.

For decades, First German Reformed sat sealed and incubating decomposition. In 2012, musician Foxy Shazam filmed a video for his song *I Like It*. It amassed 2.7 million views on YouTube. In the music video, a party is thrown in the "Church of Rock and Roll."

In 2017, the building was purchased by Joe Weiderman for the Cincinnati Rock Climbing Gym. As of 2020, the shale roof has already been replaced with more modern shingles and structural improvements have been made.

Light trails illuminate open kitchen cabinets and peeling doorways.

A peeling fresco of Jesus's crucifixion.

Vines dapple window light.

Above: A questionably constructed ladder leads to the roof.

Right: The steeple as seen from inside the attic.

Stained glass in the stairs to the steeple.

The stairs to the belfry.

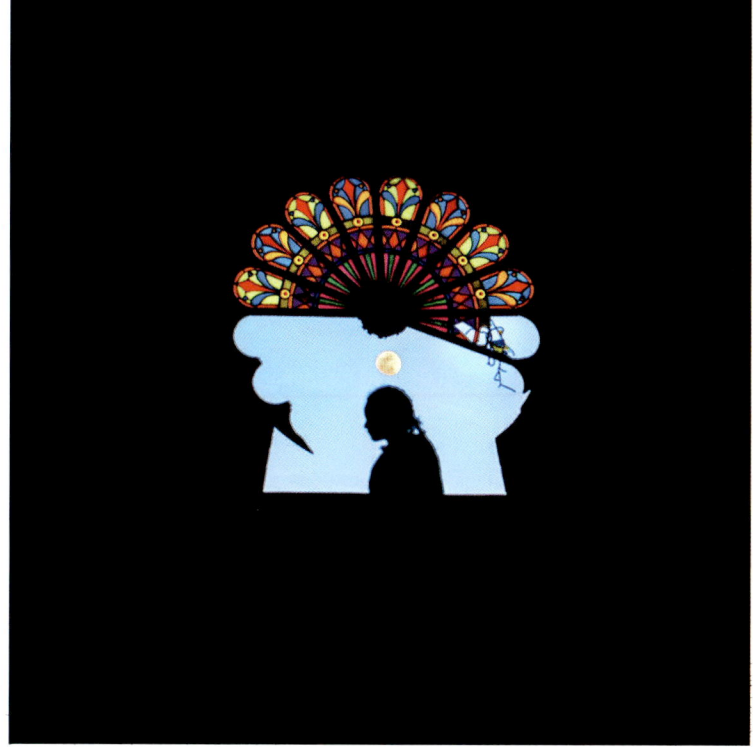

Above: The water-damaged ceiling of the chapel. A chandelier once hung here.

Right: A full moon aligns through the broken stained glass in the front of the church.

Evening light sears the back of the chapel. Grandiose curves and elegant woodwork converge to help create the mood of a holy space.

The front of the chapel. Symmetrical, painted wooden decorations once hung on either side of the pulpit.

5

AMERICANA AMUSEMENT PARK/ LESOURDSVILLE LAKE

Most of what is left of Americana Amusement Park at LeSourdsville Lake is a grave. When I first visited, most of the park had already been demolished. Still, bumper cars, arcade machines, pool toys and a Wild West saloon remained.

LeSourdsville Lake Amusement Park was created by Edgar Streifthau. In 1922, he decided to convert a former ice manufacturing facility into a park for swimming and picnics, outfitted with a 3.3-acre artificial lake. Eventually, a bandstand was built to host acts from Fats Domino to Dick Clark. In 1940, the "Screechin' Eagle" wooden roller coaster was built. By 1951, a Ferris wheel-esque "Rock-A-Plane" (which currently operates at the Coney Island of Cincinnati) and spinning "Tilt-A-Whirl" were added to the park.

Through the 70s, the park saw 600,000 people annually. In 1977, it was renamed Americana Amusement Park and became patriotic themed.

The park saw a gradual decline in patronage and funds over the next thirty years and a series of fires lead to exorbitant overhead. In 2002, after a series of owners, the park opened for its last summer.

In 2006, the lake that massive Koi fish had called home was drained. A series of roller coasters, including the seventy-year-old iconic Screechin' Eagle stood until 2011. The grounds of LeSourdsville Lake Amusement Park were sold to the City of Monroe. It is in the process of being converted to a public park and has been renamed the Bicentennial Commons Park.

Upon my last visit to the Americana Amusement Park, all that was left were a few picnic shelters and a pool house. Now, several mountains of rubble composed of concrete, rebar and twisted metal rest in the back.

The lake remains an indentation grown over by grass and weeds. A grave.

The Belle of LeSourdsville paddle boat that once took passengers on loops around the lake. The original Belle of Lesourdsville began operation in 1956.

The front door of the food court adorned with the defining blue Americana arches.

Picnic tables are stacked in one of the remaining shelters.

A cafeteria filled with overturned chairs and tables. A small stage with a painted background held performances.

Broken lamps in golden evening light. The park's lights, along with color palette and Brutalist architecture, contributed to the park's distinctly 80s aesthetic.

The *Sky Ride* pulley mechanism. *Sky Ride,* opened in 1965, was a ski-lift-esque ride that took passengers over the artificial lake.

The back of a maintenance building covered in open paint.

A double exposure of the Americana food court.

The arcade and vintage lamp posts in post-storm sunset light.

A summer sunset storm creates rough water in a swimming pool. Floating pool toys inhabited the pool along with a giant, plastic open-mouthed frog in the children's waterpark section.

An underground stretch of the haunted house. The original haunted house, named Tombstone Territory and later Logger's Run, was built in 1969.

A 1997 map of Americana Amusement park after acquisition by Coney Island Group Company.

The Parkside Inn at night. The hotel once served as a place for families visiting the park to sleep.

The front gates of LeSourdsville Lake Amusement Park.

The drained lake from mounds of rubble that once made up LeSourdsville Lake Amusement Park.

6

KENNEDY HEIGHTS JR. HIGH SCHOOL

The Kennedy Heights Junior High School felt almost post-apocalyptic. Left behind were cafeteria ovens, Erlenmeyer flasks, notes from students to teachers, and inspirational posters. It was nearly a functioning school. Yet, in the absence of custodians and elementary school cliques, something eerie remains.

Built in 1956, the 80,000-square-foot school sits in the neighborhood of Kennedy Heights. Part of the Cincinnati Public School District, Kennedy Heights Jr. High School was intended to house 830 students. In the 90s, the school adopted the Paideia education philosophy which is based around critical thinking and culture. The name of the school was changed to Shroder Paideia Jr. High School. After the construction of a new building in 2007, the school was slowly abandoned.

Piecing together the history of the school with clues found in the building felt like archeology. Through expiration dates, open file cabinets, writing on electrical boxes and forgotten photos, I began to piece together the previous life of the building.

Above: A hallway in the Kennedy Heights/Schorer Paideia Jr. High School.

Right: Green mold stains cinder blocks around Ms. Walker's room, 29 B.

Missing ceiling tiles illuminate desks. On one, a tape player/recorder.

Forgotten photos show a class of young students.

Light falls on a chalkboard.

A maze of pipes in the flooded boiler room.

Above: The Kennedy Heights' 500-seat auditorium. Record players, music stands, props and curtains remain on the stage.

Left: The auditorium stairs and a row of lockers.

An overhead projector surrounded by lockers.

A blackboard lit by evening light in the music room. On the opposite wall, a bookcase held stacks of sheet music and a teacher's button-downs.

Above: Beakers and an Erlenmeyer flask in a science room. A projector screen hangs over the chalkboard.

Left: A box of plastic human organs at the bottom of a set of stairs.

Right: Headphones on water-damaged tiles.

Below: A mound of crayons sits against lockers in the Kennedy Heights Junior High School.

57

Left: Once-teal doors peel and flake.

Below: The men's gym locker room. One locker reads: "Terrance." Another: "Antonio." The sink pipes have been scrapped for metal.

The Woodford Paideia Academy gymnasium, once home to the Jaguars. Scattered on the wood floor: a hula hoop, fallen bird nests, a desk, makeshift tape game lines and wrestling mats.

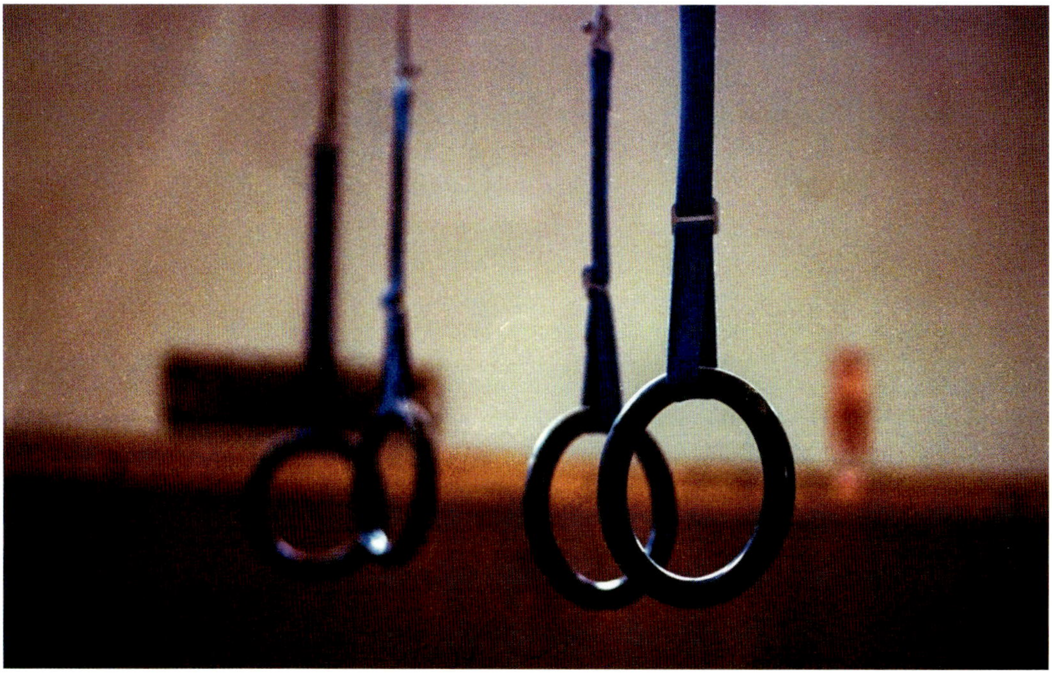

Gymnastic rings hang from the ceiling of the gymnasium.

Floor scooters left on the Woodford Paideia gym floor.

Booths in the cafeteria of Kennedy Heights Jr. High School. Notes from children, books and homework rest in a corner on the other side of the room.

7

LOVELAND PREDESTINARIAN BAPTIST CHURCH

The darkness of a burnt-out basement peeks through a hole in moldy shag carpet stretched over decrepit floorboards. Used needles and scorched songbooks scatter the humble Predestinarian Baptist Church in the city of Loveland.

In 1892, Philip Roller sold the land to build a four-room chapel. The predominantly black church operated for 107 years. Towards the end of the church's life, it was purchased and renamed the Mt. Calvary Church. It passed pastorship until Reverend John Mackey died in 2001. Soon after, the church was abandoned.

In 2011, the city of Loveland acquired the church and considered demolition. Citizens successfully rallied at a city council meeting to delay the church's destruction. Sometime after 2012, a fire destroyed part of the floor and many of the pews. The roof has collapsed in the back of the chapel and foliage now peeks through rubble and shingles.

Light streams through the front of Loveland Predestinarian Baptist Church/Mt. Calvary Church.

Evening light illuminates pews and moldy carpet.

A torn painting of Jesus. It once read INRI, an acronym that translates to "Jesus the Nazarene, King of the Jews."

The preacher's vantage of burnt pews. A charred Bible rests on the pulpit.

A fire-scorched songbook sits opened to "It's Just Like Heaven." The book rests on a dusty Wurlitzer electric organ.

The back room of the Predestinarian Baptist Church.

The Loveland Predestinarian Baptist Church exterior.

8

QUANTUM CHEMICALS RESEARCH DIVISION

In New Age steel font: lettering that once read "RESEARCH DIVISION." Trees and shrubbery push through crumbling concrete. Overgrowth snakes around shattered reinforced glass. Flame arrestors cover roofs and a giant pulley and outdoor cages with toxic substance warnings create an industrial dystopia. Boats, cars without engines and broken windshields fill every corner.

Partially constructed in 1950, the exact history of the lot in Carthage is hazy. In 1988, Quantum Chemicals purchased the site. Quantum Chemicals is a petrochemical refining company that claims to be the largest manufacturer of polyethylene in the country. Polyethylene is a chemical used to make products such as plastic grocery bags, shampoo bottles, and children's toys. The company utilized the site until around 2009. In 2013, Quantum Chemicals sold the property. It has since fallen to disuse.

Interestingly, the nearly six-acre site is currently zoned for nursing home and hospital use.

The now-overgrown exterior of Quantum Chemicals Research Division.

A Triumph TR6, manufactured between 1968 and 1976, collects dust.

A cracked window reflects over a moldy room filled with scrap car parts.

A panel of various meters measuring and controlling operations such as isobutane flow, loop reactor press pressure, and the vulcan block valve. Many of the meters contain charts that have stopped abruptly.

One of the many loudspeakers placed throughout the facility that served as a safety precaution.

An explosion-proof 30-pound Western Electric model 2520 Telephone. Introduced in 1974, the line of industrial telephones was manufactured to survive hazardous atmospheres.

A set of rusty Quantum Chemicals stairs.

The Longview Asylum, built in 1856, at one point housed 3,000 mentally ill patients. The hospital operated over capacity and under budget. On some of what is now the grounds of the abandoned Quantum Chemicals Research Division building, hundreds if not thousands of patients died of starvation and malnutrition. The asylum operated under various names for about 125 years before closure in the 1980s.

For a handful of years, the Longview Asylum buildings stood abandoned. In that time, patient records, X-Rays, dental casts—remnants of over a hundred years of caring for and hiding away the mentally ill—remained. The hospital buildings were mostly demolished by the early 90s. Quantum Chemicals converted some of the buildings and new facilities were also constructed. Now, there is no trace of the asylum buildings.

Currently, the lot is again abandoned. Rows of enormous fume hoods are exposed to the elements. In a dark, water-logged basement, books filled with gas chromatography records are eaten by mold.

In the lot there is evidence of what can only be presumed to be a chop shop where ill-obtained vehicles are dismantled and sold for parts. Old car hoods are scattered throughout the overgrowth and luxury sports cars collect dust under rusty reactor tanks.

Flexible tubing arcs out of an electrical box.

A boombox and bicycle sit on top of a third-generation Pontiac Firebird.

A doorway to a room filled with reactors, pipes, fume hoods, rust, mold and broken glass.

A batch reactor for chemical production. An agitator (top component) dropped chemicals into the metal chasm about 20 feet deep.

Vinyl records rest on a fume hood. Some held library cards with a final check out date in the 1940s. Why they were in one building along with family photo albums is unclear.

Light passes through a mid-1980s Monte Carlo in the Quantum Chemicals parking lot.

9

THE CROSLEY BUILDING

In the Camp Washington neighborhood, an Art Deco castle crumbles into rust and broken glass. Towering over trainyards and city lights, the so-called "Nation's Station" once rose above America from the Crosley Building. The rooms that housed innovations ranging from the first Major League Baseball broadcast to the Apollo Lunar Lander are quiet now.

Powel Crosley Jr.'s luxury car line was struggling. The young inventor was due for a new product. His timely guess? An inexpensive radio. In 1921, his seven-dollar invention helped foster a boom that grounded the radio as a household staple.

The inexpensive components of Crosley's Harko model radios demanded a stronger signal. Powel Crosley Jr. founded his own radio station, named WLW. By 1928, WLW constructed the first and only 500,000-watt stations upon special permission from the U.S. government. The signal was so strong that farmers near the Mason transmitter reported hearing the station in their barbed-wire fences. Much of the United States received WLW, leading to the branding of "The Nation's Station." The same year, Crosley purchased the WSAI station from the U.S. Playing Card company. Rapid growth lead to a need for new recording studios and offices.

Designed by Cincinnati-based architecture firm Samuel Hannaford and Sons to resemble a radio set, the 330,000-square-foot Crosley building once held five studios behind ornate, 800-pound doors. The top two floors accommodated a full orchestra. Inside the iconic tower, Powell Crosley Jr.'s office was outfitted with stained glass and a shower. The bottom seven floors held research and development for Crosley's radios, cars and appliances. On top of the roof, two enormous radio towers served as a link to the WLW transmitter. At the height of the Crosley empire, the company was the single largest employer in Cincinnati with a 7,000-person payroll.

The exterior of the Crosley Building.

Puddles turn the industrial floor to a mirror.

A skywalk connected the main Crosley building to an adjoining warehouse until the 1937 Ohio River flood. High water lead to a gas tank explosion that burned the warehouse to the ground. The previous location of the ornate walkway is now sealed with concrete.

The Crosley company was bought by Aviation Company (AVCO) in 1946. WLW left the Crosley building and AVCO began to use the space as a design and manufacturing plant. Inside, the first disc brakes, fridges with door shelves, technology for America's first all-color TV station (WLWT) and plated armor used on the Apollo Lunar Module were developed.

In the late 70s, AVCO left the Crosley building and Cincinnati. The site switched hands several times, operating eventually as a warehouse. In 2006, the Crosley building was abandoned and six years later it was condemned. In 2014, the structure was added to the National Registry of Historic Places.

The Crosley record/radio company still carries Powel Crosley Jr.'s name today. The Cincinnati Red's Crosley Field was demolished in 1972. WLW is now a talk radio station owned by iHeartMedia.

Today, the Crosley building looms over the Queen City's warehouses and factories a fallen castle. The ornate woodwork of Crosley's office has toppled and the stained glass surrounding his desk has cracked. Powel Crosley's kingdom has come and gone.

Evening light spills through broken windows onto a metal dolly cart.

Broken siding sits on a peeling stairwell. Mounds of plaster and paint dust coat the steps.

Left: Dirty tiles scatter the floor of a bathroom.

Below: A flooded and overgrown landing with a rusty roof vent turbine.

Right: A Cleaver Brooks industrial boiler.

Below: Peeling doors on the floor where WLW's studios once recorded.

Above: Glass tangled in a telephone switchboard.

Left: A broken and rickety ladder leads to the top of the tower. On the right, an enormous water tank.

Above: A skeletal billboard looks out to a busy highway. It once held a neon sign reading "WLW."

Right: The iconic Crosley Tower.

10

PETERS CARTRIDGE FACTORY

A brick tower and smokestack jut out of the Little Miami River valley. They are decorated with blue-and-white tilework reading the letter "P." Held in place by vines and reinforced concrete, the Peters Cartridge factory's shattered windows and decrepit doors allow a glimpse into a world bygone.

In 1877, Gershom Moore Peters' father-in-law, Joseph Warren King, founded the Great Western Powder Works. As the business grew, his company built the town of Kings Mills. After King's death, Peters continued to expand a series of munition factories along the river and formed Peters Cartridge Company.

With World War I approaching, the demand for ammunition boomed. In 1916, Peters Cartridge Company constructed a new plant to supply shotgun casings for the Russian Empire and the United Kingdom. The new factory featured an indoor shooting range, ballistic analysis lab, powerhouse, machine shop, furnace room and buildings designated for casing assembly. At one time, a second skywalk extended over Grandin Road to a warehouse. A hydroelectric dam provided power for the plant.

Perhaps most architecturally striking is the shot tower. In the top of the tower, molten lead was poured through a screen and down a 200-foot shaft where it formed into round pellets. A water basin collected and cooled the shotgun pellets at the bottom.

Above left: The Peters Cartridge factory skywalk and tower.

Above right: Intricate prairie-style polychrome tilework decorates the walkway joining two buildings. The opposite building was used for loading shells and held offices on the top floors.

A concrete platform surrounded by standing water and rickety rails leads to overgrowth.

Vibrant decay in a stairwell.

A mangled bicycle rests among tires, chairs and hubcaps in a basement room.

Looking down through the top of the shot tower. It is one of seven remaining in America.

A light passes through a basement boiler room painted bright with mold and rust.

Chaotic window frames and vines overlay twisted machinery and ice.

The elevator shaft that once moved machinery and workers up the tower.

The elevator's pulley mechanism located on the roof.

89

Sunset from the rooftop of Peters Cartridge factory. The Virginia creeper-twined tower and 250-foot smokestack bear a tile "P" after Gershom Moore Peters. The Italian Renaissance-style watchtower was tiled until an earthquake in 1968.

The interior of the tower.

Working at the Peters Cartridge factory was not without hazard. Ten explosions killed twenty-one people. One 1942 explosion was heard 30 miles away. Factories were spaced apart to avoid chain reaction fires/explosions.

In 1934, Remington Arms bought the Peters Cartridge factory for World War II. By 1946, Columbia Records bought the facility to produce vinyl records. Two years later, Columbia passed the plant to the Seagram distillery company. By the mid 80s, the building was abandoned beyond partial warehouse use.

Out of death: new life. Mold ate wood doors. Rolled steel window frames rusted and time wore cracks in the roof. A tree grew through the middle of a tall-ceilinged loading room. The distinct smell of decay claimed the factory.

In 2009, the EPA deemed the factory a hazardous waste site. The Dupont chemical company was held responsible due to their prior ownership of the site where lead, copper, mercury, boiler ash and slag were found at dangerous levels. A $5 million cleanup is said to have restored the 71-acre parcel of land to a safe condition.

In 2014, developers Bloomfield/Schon began to convert the dilapidated factory into a brewery, cafe, private event area and 135 apartments.

While Peters Cartridge factory loses the beauty of its decay, it hardly matters. Someday, the earth will dissolve and disperse fallen tiles. Vines will suffocate bricks and rain will wash glass into river sand. A spring will come when the sycamores and underbrush that Gershom Peters cleared over 100 years ago will again begin to bud. In constant flux: life and a time before.

Evening light fans over moss and mildew in the Peters Cartridge Factory's rifle range, where ammunition was tested in an enclosed space.

Virginia creeper and poison ivy grow into the basement.

The interior of the Peters Cartridge factory during use as a warehouse. Engine parts, machinery and forklifts scatter the floor.

The corrugated ceiling of the furnace room.

A catwalk above the furnace room. It is outfitted with pulleys that supplied materials for the ovens.

Piping and machinery that supplied power to the munitions factory.

Above: The four-story coal-burning furnaces used to melt lead and brass to make shell casings.

Right: New growth consumes a dying tree as the moon rises over Peters Cartridge Factory.

ABOUT THE AUTHOR

SAMUEL WRIGHT SMITH is a photographer, filmmaker, and animator located in Cincinnati and New York City. Smith was surrounded by visual art from a young age, and it quickly became his life. Garnering experience as a journalistic writer and photographer through high school, his interest only grew.

He has made it his goal to share images that are both personal and universal. At only nineteen years old, Sam Smith aims to continue on a path where he can share light and experience with others through art. Smith currently attends New York University and is studying film. To see more of Sam Smith's work, visit www.samwsmith.net and follow @samwsmith33 on Instagram.